Spanish *Cooking*

Delicious & Authentic Recipes

susaeta

Contents

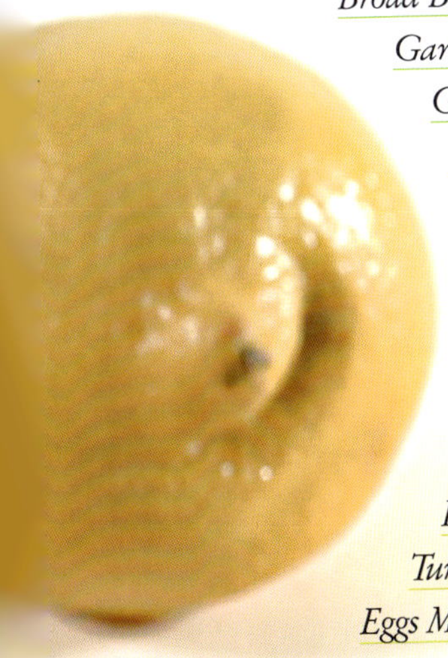

Spanish Cooking

One of the most attractive aspects of Spanish culture is without any doubt its cuisine.

Throughout time Spanish gastronomy has incorporated influences since the days of the Romans, the Jews, the Arabs and the New World.

The cooks of the Iberian Peninsula learned the techniques to make bread and brew beer from the Egyptians, and it was the Phoenicians who brought and planted olive trees, olive oil today being the star ingredient of Spanish cooking.

The Moors and Berbers stayed in Spain for eight hundred years, and their influence on Spanish gastronomy was decisive in the appearance of the varied regional cooking that we enjoy today.

The New World brought corn, potatoes, beans and peppers, which we learned how to dry and grind and thus make paprika, a condiment that is a basic ingredient of many regional Spanish recipes.

Spanish gastronomy can be basically divided into four groups, according to the climate: Mediterranean, Southern, Central and Northern.

Garnishing Tips

STEP-BY-STEP

Garnishing Spanish dishes is really quite simple and straightforward, many dishes making do with just a sprig of parsley. However, that does not mean that we cannot prepare our appetizing menus with less sobriety than in the past.

Contrary to what many people may think, sea bass in a salt crust baked in the oven does not dry the fish nor does it make it too salty. In this first tip, on how to serve sea bass or any other fish in a salt crust, in just a few steps we will show you how to present the dish in a way that will certainly impress your dinner guests.

Carrots can easily be cut in many different ways to garnish any dish, in this case, a three-petalled flower, which can be used to garnish either fish or meat recipes.

Lemons also offer a great range of possibilities for dressing. On the following page there is one which can be used for both desserts and fish.

Sea Bass in a Salt Crust

1. Wash the fish, but do not remove either scales or guts so that the salt will not penetrate inside the fish. Arrange a layer of salt on an oven tray, giving it the form of a fish.

2. Place the fish on top of the salt.

3. Put another layer of salt over the fish until it is completely covered. Sprinkle with a little water to make it easier to shape the salt around the fish, always giving it the shape of a fish.

4. Using a tablespoon, mark the scales, eye and the tail. Place the tray in the oven. When ready, separate the fillets according to the recipe.

Carrot Flower Garnish

1. Peel and wash carrot.
2. Cut the piece you're going to use to make the flower from the thicker part, in the shape of a regular triangle seen from the carrot base.
3. Once you've cut the triangle, remove the edges and discard them. Depending on the size of flower you wish to make, cut the petals at the same level and remove the inner part.
4. Cut off the rest of the base so that the "flower" will be able to stand flat on any surface.

Lemon Spiral Garnish

1. Wash the lemon and cut off one end.
2. Using a special cutter, peel the lemon, being careful the rind is cut in one piece and that it is still attached to the unsliced end.
3. Arrange the lemon spiral as you wish.
   The final result can be used to decorate fish or desserts.

Hors D'oeuvres

Cold Almond & Garlic Soup

(Ajoblanco)

200 g raw almonds

2 cloves of garlic

10 tablesp. olive oil

Salt

150 g breadcrumb

1 tablesp. vinegar

1 $1/2$ litres of water

Sweet green grapes

2 slices of bread

METHOD FOR 4

1. Put the breadcrumb in a bowl with water until it becomes soft and spongy.
2. So that the almonds will be easy to peel, boil some water in a saucepan and place a colander with the almonds over it for a few minutes. Peel them.
3. Peel the cloves of garlic. Put them in the blender together with the almonds, salt and a little water. Mix into a fine paste.
4. Drain the breadcrumb well and add to the blender. Beat again, adding the oil gradually (as if you were making mayonnaise).
5. When the mixture is well blended, add 1 tablespoonful of vinegar. Continue to add the rest of the water little by little.
6. Put the cream in a tureen and refrigerate for at least 2 hours.
7. Cut the bread into slices 1 cm thick and toast in the oven.
8. Serve the *ajoblanco* with grapes and croutons.

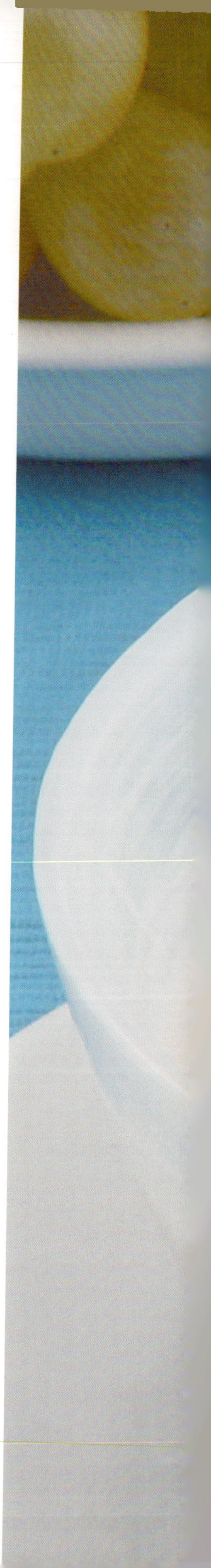

Ajoblanco

Fried Breadcrumbs with Bacon

(Migas extremeñas)

Stale loaf of bread

200 g fat bacon

2 dried peppers

3 cloves of garlic

Olive oil

Salt

METHOD FOR 4

1. Soak the dried peppers in water.
2. Cut the bread loaf in two and then in horizontal slices. Dice it into pieces the size of a hazelnut.
3. Put the diced bread on a very clean, damp cloth. Tie the cloth and leave to rest.
4. Dice the bacon and the peppers (previously soaked and drained).
5. Peel and crush the cloves of garlic.
6. Put oil in a large, shallow pan. When the oil is hot, fry the garlic. When it starts turning golden, remove from heat. Add the diced bread, stirring all the time.
7. Add the salt before adding the bacon and the pepper.
8. Stir well until the bread has absorbed all the bacon juice. Fry until golden. Serve hot.

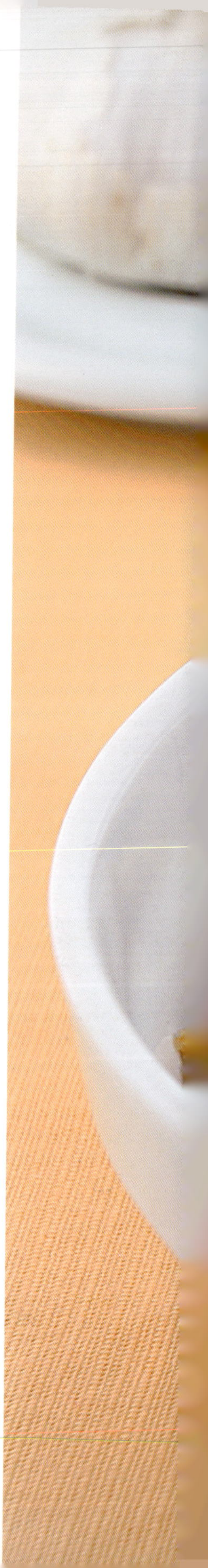

Migas extremeñas

Octopus, Galician-Style

(Pulpo a la gallega)

1 kg octopus

12 cups of water

1 bay leaf

1/2 onion

4-6 grains of black pepper

Parsley

1/2 cup of olive oil

1 tablesp. paprika

Freshly-ground black pepper

Unrefined salt

METHOD FOR 4

1. Clean the octopus well, gut it and discard all waste including the eyes. Cut off the tentacle tips.
2. Soften the octopus meat by beating it against a hard surface.
3. Put the water into a large saucepan. Bring to the boil. Submerge the octopus and take it out immediately. Repeat this procedure a further two times. Remove the octopus and set aside.
4. Bring the water to the boil again. Add the bay leaf, the 1/2 onion (not cut), the grains of pepper, the parsley and a pinch of salt.
5. Put the octopus back into the saucepan. Cover with a lid. Cook over a very low heat until the octopus is tender.
6. When the octopus is ready, drain and set aside to cool. Slice the tentacles. Cut the rest of the octopus into small pieces.
7. Mix the olive oil, the paprika, the salt and the pepper in a bowl.
8. Finally, arrange the octopus pieces on a plate and season with the previous mixture.

1 kg potatoes

½ kg of tomatoes

1 chilli pepper

½ glass of white wine

1 tablesp. flour

Hot paprika

Olive oil

Salt

Water

A pinch of sugar

Potatoes with Spicy Tomato Sauce

(Patatas bravas)

METHOD FOR 4

1. Peel and wash the potatoes. Cut into cubes.
2. Fry or boil, according to preference.
3. Wash, peel and deseed the tomatoes.
4. Heat the olive oil in a frying pan. Sauté the tomatoes together with the chilli pepper and a pinch of sugar (to take some of the acidity out of the tomatoes).
5. When cooked, add the white wine, the spoonful of flour and a little hot paprika. Stir well until the sauce is well blended.
6. Remove the chilli pepper. Season the sauce with salt.
7. Put the potatoes on a plate and drizzle with the sauce.
8. If the sauce is too thick, a little water may be added.

Scrambled Eggs with Courgettes

and Ham

1 onion or 2 shallots

1 green pepper

$1/2$ sweet pepper

1 ripe tomato

1 courgette

5-6 eggs

4 slices cured ham

4 tablesp. olive oil

Salt

Chives

METHOD FOR 4

1. Chop the onion finely. Wash the green pepper and the $1/2$ sweet pepper. Chop peppers finely.
2. Scald the tomato a few minutes in hot water so as to remove the skin easily. Then deseed and chop.
3. Wash and peel the courgette. Dice in small pieces.
4. Heat the oil in a pan. Sauté all the ingredients over a low heat until soft. Season.
5. Beat the eggs with a pinch of salt. Pour into the pan, stirring continuously with a wooden spoon, until the egg sets.
6. May be served as in the picture: shape the cooked scrambled egg mixture with a mould and garnish with sprigs of chive.
7. Serve on a plate with slices of ham.

Scrambled Eggs with Courgettes and Ham

Clams in Parsley Sauce

$^1/_2$ kg clams

3 cloves of garlic

1 chilli pepper

4 tablesp. olive oil

1 tablesp. flour

1 small glass of white wine

Parsley

Salt

METHOD FOR 4

1. Clean the clams very well to get rid of any sand. Discard those that have broken shells or have not closed when cleaning.
2. Peel and finelyslice the cloves of garlic.
3. Heat oil in a pan and fry the garlic with a pinch of salt.
4. When it starts to turn slightly golden, add the chilli pepper.
5. Add 1 or 2 tablespoonfuls of flour and stir well.
6. Pour in the glass of white wine. Keep on stirring and adding water until you get the right consistency.
7. Wash and finely chop the parsley. Add to sauce.
8. When the sauce starts to simmer, add the clams.
9. Wait until they open up. Serve hot.

Clams in Parsley Sauce

Broad Beans with Ham

2 kg broad beans
200 g cured ham
1 onion
1 small glass of olive oil
Salt

METHOD FOR 4

1. Remove the beans from pods and rinse.
2. Heat the oil in a frying pan. Sauté the diced ham. Set aside.
3. Finely chop the onion.
4. In the same oil, sauté the onion until soft.
5. Add the beans (drained).
6. Cover and cook over a low heat for 30 minutes until the beans are tender.
7. When nearly cooked, add the salt and the sautéed ham.

1 kg prawns

$1/2$ chilli pepper

4 cloves of garlic

3 tablesp. olive oil

Parsley

Salt

Garlic Prawns

(Gambas al ajillo)

METHOD FOR 4

1. Peel the uncooked prawns, leaving the tails whole. Be careful they don't split.
2. Peel and chop the garlic. Cut the $1/2$ chilli pepper into rings.
3. Rinse and finely chop the parsley.
4. Heat the oil in a frying pan. Sauté the garlic until golden, being careful it doesn't burn.
5. Add the sliced chilli pepper, the chopped parsley and the prawns.
6. Season and toss for a few minutes over a high heat, moving the pan all the time.
7. The prawns may be served in the same pan to keep them warm.

Gazpacho

100 g bread

500 g ripe red tomatoes

100 g green peppers

2 cloves of garlic

14 tablesp. olive oil

2 tablesp. vinegar

Salt

1 litre of cold water

100 g breadcrumb

METHOD FOR 4

1. Put the breadcrumb in a bowl with water.
2. Wash, peel and chop the tomatoes.
3. Wash the peppers and cut them into strips to be able to crush them better.
4. Peel and chop the garlic.
5. In a blender, mix the cloves of garlic, the pepper and a little salt.
6. Next, add the tomatoes and the breadcrumb (well drained).
7. When the mixture is well blended, add the oil gradually. Thin the gazpacho with a little water. Strain well to get rid of all the bits.
8. Add the rest of the water. Check seasoning and add the vinegar.
9. For the garnish, dice the green pepper, the tomatoes and the bread.
10. Serve the gazpacho very cold, with the garnish separately.

Gazpacho

Stuffed Grilled Mussels

1 kg mussels

80 g butter

2-3 tablesp. flour

1/2 litre milk

1/2 lemon

Black ground pepper

Tabasco sauce

Breadcrumbs

Salt

2 eggs

METHOD FOR 4

1. Clean the mussels well and put them in cold water several times to get rid of any sand.
2. Once clean, cook them in water and lemon juice until they all open up. Drain and remove the empty shell. Keep half a glass of the water used for cooking the mussels and set aside.
3. Melt the butter in another pan. Add the flour, stirring well with a wooden spoon for a few minutes. Make sure the flour doesn't brown.
4. Keep on stirring while you pour in the milk and the glass of water used for cooking the mussels, taking care that no lumps are formed. When the mixture has a fine consistency, season with salt, a little ground pepper and a dash of Tabasco.
5. Leave to cook a further 10 or 15 minutes, stirring continuously so that the sauce doesn't burn. Cut up the mussels and add them to the white sauce. The sauce is ready when it comes off the sides of the pan.
6. Leave the mixture to cool and thicken. Fill the mussel shells with the sauce.
7. Coat the filled shells with egg and breadcrumbs. Fry a few minutes in a pan with very hot oil.

Stuffed Grilled Mussels

First Courses

Chick-pea and Meat Stew

(Cocido madrileño)

500 g chick-peas
1 kg cabbage
½ kg carrots
4 medium-sized potatoes
½ kg meat (shank or shin)
2 cow bones
½ hen's breast
1 chorizo sausage
1 gammon bone
1 small ham bone
1 black pudding with rice
150 g fresh fat bacon
250 g noodles
Salt

A little oil
2 cloves of garlic

METHOD FOR 4

1. The day before, soak the chick-peas in warm water with a little salt.
2. Fill a large pan with cold water. Add the meat, bones and fat bacon. Bring to the boil and add the chick-peas (drained). Cover and simmer for one hour.
3. Skim the stock and add the hen's breast and the chorizo sausage. Cover the pot again. Leave to cook for another hour. Season. Add the peeled carrots (cut in half lengthwise). Take out some stock for making soup, always refilling the pan with hot water.
4. Cover the pan again. Cook for another 30 minutes and then add the potatoes (peeled and washed).
5. Simmer for a further 30 minutes until the chickpeas are cooked.
6. Chop and rinse the cabbage and cook it separately. Before serving, heat a little oil in a frying pan, sauté the garlic and then toss the cabbage.
7. Cook or fry the black pudding separately, according to taste.
8. Make a soup by boiling the stock (previously reserved). Add more stock from the pan, but leaving some in the pan so that the ingredients won't go dry. Add the noodles.
9. Boil for 15 minutes. Serve the broth separately in a tureen.
10. Cut the meat, chorizo, bacon, black pudding and hen meat and arrange on a serving dish.
11. Serve the chick-peas, vegetables and potatoes on another dish.

Cocido madrileño

Green Asparagus Soup

1 bunch of fresh green asparagus

2 eggs

2 cloves of garlic

Sweet paprika

Bread

Olive oil

Vinegar

Salt

METHOD FOR 4

1. Wash the asparagus, discarding the hard part and cut in equal-sized pieces.
2. Cover with water. Add salt and bring to the boil. Cook until the asparagus is tender.
3. Heat the oil in a pan. Sauté the chopped garlic until golden. Remove from pan and set aside.
4. In the same oil, fry a slice of bread. Remove from pan and set aside.
5. With a blender, crush the garlic and the bread. Blend it well with a little of the water from cooking the asparagus.
6. Add the mixture to the stock and add a spoonful of paprika.
7. Allow to boil for a few seconds until the broth thickens a little.
8. Beat 2 eggs, pour them into the soup. Add a spoonful of vinegar and bring to the boil.

Green Asparagus Soup

Beans Stewed with Sausage & Bacon

(Fabada asturiana)

500 g beans *(fabes)*

2 chorizo sausages

2 black puddings

100 g cured ham

300 g fat bacon

100 g cooked ham

15 g rancid bacon

Salt

Pepper

Saffron

METHOD FOR 4

1. The previous night, put the beans in water to soak.
2. The next day, put them in a pan with cold water along with all the ingredients except the rancid bacon and the saffron. Bring to the boil over a low heat.
3. Crush the rancid bacon and the saffron with a pestle and mortar. Set aside.
4. Cover the pan and simmer over a low heat for 3 hours.
5. When the beans are half cooked, add the mixture made in the mortar, blended with a little of the stock from cooking the beans.
6. When the beans are tender, season and serve.

150 g pork ribs
100 g pork sausages
250 g ripe tomatoes
400 g thick noodles
½ litre of meat stock
1 onion
1 clove of garlic
Olive oil
Parsley
Pepper
Salt

Pork Noodles, Catalan-Style

METHOD FOR 4

1. Chop the ribs. Remove the string from the sausages.
2. Peel and chop the garlic.
3. Wash and grate the tomatoes.
4. Fry the pork ribs in oil in a heatproof earthenware dish. When they start to turn golden, add the chopped garlic and the grated tomatoes. Leave to cook slowly for 10 minutes.
5. Pour in the hot stock and cook for a further 10 minutes.
6. Add the noodles and season. Stir and cook for 12 minutes.
7. If the noodles are still uncooked, some more water may be added, provided it is hot.
8. Serve on individual plates, garnished with chopped parsley.

Tuna Fish & Potato Stew

(Marmitako)

1 $1/2$ kg fresh tuna fish
1 kg potatoes
6 green peppers
1 dl of olive oil
1 leek
3 onions
3 dried peppers
250 g ripe tomatoes
2 cloves of garlic
1 chilli pepper
Paprika
Parsley
Salt

METHOD FOR 4

1. Scald the dried peppers and take out the pulp.
2. Put $1/2$ litre of water in a large pan. Add the tuna fish head and tail, the sliced leek, 2 finely-diced green peppers and a whole onion (peeled).
3. Bring to the boil and simmer for 30 minutes. Strain the stock and set to one side.
4. Heat the olive oil in a frying pan and sauté the remaining onions (chopped).
5. When the onions are golden, add the following to the pan: the pulp of the dried peppers, the peeled, deseeded and chopped tomatoes, the cloves of garlic and the chopped parsley.
6. Cook for 15 minutes over a low heat.
7. Add a slice of chilli pepper and the paprika. Stir quickly.
8. Add the rest of the green peppers (finely chopped) and the potatoes (diced).
9. Stir well.
10. Cover the potatoes with the boiling stock.
11. When the potatoes are cooked, add the tuna fish, (previously rinsed and chopped). Season and stir carefully.
12. Simmer for 8 minutes. Leave to rest a little before serving.

Marmitako

Eggs Mayonnaise

9 eggs

2 cans of tuna fish in olive oil

3 tablesp. tomato purée

1 lemon

Salt

Sweet pepper

METHOD FOR 4

1 Hard boil 8 of the eggs (10-12 minutes).

2 Rinse the hard-boiled eggs under a cold tap. When they are cold, peel. Cut into halves lengthwise and remove yolks. Some of the yolks are to be used for making the filling and others for garnishing.

3 Mix the 2 cans of tuna fish with the tomato purée and yolks. Fill the eggs (the space left from removing the yolks) with this mixture. Arrange them face down on a serving dish.

4 To make the mayonnaise, break the remaining egg in a bowl. Add the olive oil and salt. Beat to a thick sauce, adding the juice of 1/2 lemon at the end. Check seasoning.

5 Pour the mayonnaise over the eggs on the dish. May be garnished with egg yolk and strips of sweet pepper.

Eggs Mayonnaise

Stewed Beans

with Pig's Ear

500 g beans
200 g pig's ear
100 g chorizo sausage
1 ham bone
1 tomato
1 green pepper
1 onion
1 clove of garlic
Tomato purée
1 teasp. flour
3 tablesp. olive oil
1/2 teasp. sweet paprika
Salt

METHOD FOR 4

1. The day before, put the beans to soak in cold water.
2. Clean the pig's ear very carefully, then chop.
3. Chop the green pepper and the tomato.
4. Peel and cut the onion, keeping a little for frying.
5. Drain the beans and put them in a pan with cold water. Bring to the boil and cook over a low heat for 2 hours together with the pig's ear, the sausage, the ham bone, the pepper, the tomato and the whole clove of garlic.
6. Meanwhile, heat the oil in a pan. Sauté the chopped onion. Add the spoonful of flour, the sweet paprika, the tomato purée and the salt. Cook over a low heat for a few minutes and remove from heat.
7. When the beans are cooked, add the tomato sauce. Stir well and leave to cook for a further 10 minutes.

1 $1/2$ kg potatoes

1 red pepper

1 large ripe tomato

2 cloves of garlic

1 bay leaf

$1/2$ tablesp. paprika

4 tablesp. olive oil

Salt

Stewed Potatoes

& Peppers

METHOD FOR 4

1. Peel, rinse and cut potatoes into thick rounds.
2. Peel, deseed and crush the tomatoes.
3. Wash and dice the pepper.
4. Peel and crush the garlic.
5. Heat the oil in a pan. Sauté the pepper and tomato. Add the potatoes. Stir a few minutes and sprinkle with salt and paprika.
6. Cover the potatoes with water. Add the crushed garlic and the bay leaf. Cook until the potatoes are ready and the stock thick.

Paella

250 g fresh prawns

250 g mussels

1 cup of olive oil

1 large chicken, chopped

1 green pepper

2 ripe tomatoes

2 cloves of garlic

1/4 kg small clams

1/2 kg or 2 cups of rice

4 cups of water

Saffron

Yellow food colouring

4 king prawns

100 g peas

Sweet pepper

Salt

1 lemon

METHOD FOR 4

1. Peel the shrimps. Make stock by boiling the shells in water. Strain and set aside.
2. Put the mussels in a pan with very little water. Cook until they open up. Set aside.
3. Rinse and cut the peppers into strips. Wash and peel the tomatoes.
4. Peel and roughly chop the garlic. Set to one side.
5. Heat the oil in the pan in which you will make the rice (preferably a paella pan).
6. When the oil is very hot, add the chicken (chopped in medium-sized pieces). Fry, turning occasionally, until golden brown.
7. Add the green pepper, taking care it doesn't burn, then the clams until they all open up. When the pepper starts to turn golden, add the tomato pulp. Mix well until you have a jam consistency.
8. Add the garlic and before it starts to turn brown, add the 2 cups of rice. Sauté everything for a few seconds so that the rice will take the flavour of the vegetables.
9. Add 4 cups of the stock from cooking the shrimp shells, the saffron, a little yellow food colouring and stir.
10. On top of the rice, arrange the shrimps, the cooked mussels, the peas, the sweet pepper and the king prawns.
11. Cook until the water is absorbed. Cover the paella with clean cloth and leave to rest for 10 minutes.
12. Serve garnished with lemon wedges and aliolli sauce.

Paella

Lentils

with Muscatel Wine

500 g lentils

1 ham bone

2 leeks

1 onion

150 g mushrooms

2 tomatoes

2 black puddings

Salt

5 dl of olive oil

A few drops of anisette liquor

1 glass of muscatel wine

METHOD FOR 4

1. The evening before, soak the lentils in water.
2. Drain the lentils and put them in a pan with lukewarm water together with the ham bone.
3. Wash the leeks well, discarding the green part. Cut into fine slices. Peel and slice the onion.
4. Clean and chop the mushrooms.
5. Peel the tomato, discarding the seeds and chop.
6. Slice the black puddings.
7. Heat the oil in a frying pan. Sauté all the ingredients, taking care that they don't burn.
8. When the lentils are nearly ready, add the sautéed mixture. Cook for about 10 minutes. Check seasoning.
9. Remove the lentils from the heat and add a few drops of anisette liquor and a glass of muscatel wine.

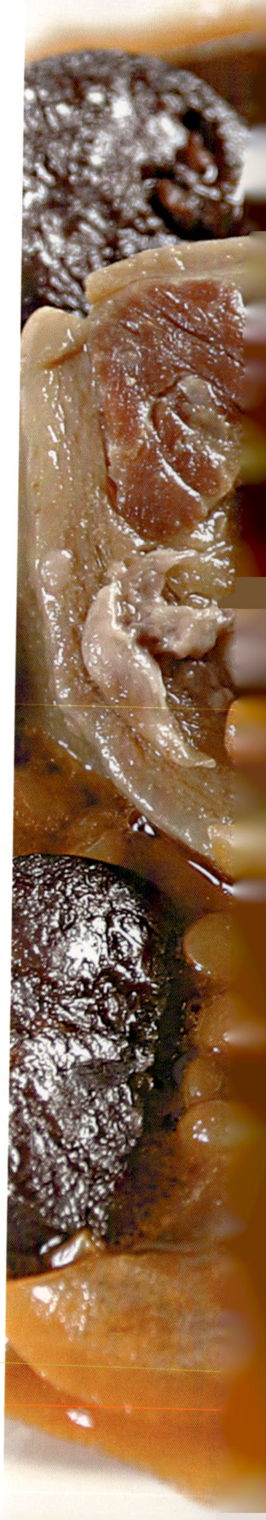

Lentils with Muscatel Wine

Meat Dishes

Roast Lamb

4 small shoulders of suckling lamb

1 kg potatoes

1 dl olive oil

Black pepper

10 cloves of garlic

Salt

1 sprig of rosemary

2 small glasses of water

Juice of 2 lemons

Water

METHOD FOR 4

1. Choose small shoulders of lamb and make several gashes. Season.
2. Peel and roughly slice the cloves of garlic.
3. Put the sliced garlic in the gashes made to flavour the lamb when roasting.
4. Place the shoulders of lamb in an oven dish. Sprinkle with the lemon juice, the oil, the sprig of rosemary and a glass of water.
5. Bake for 20 minutes at 180°C. Open the oven to add another glass of water, taking care not to pour it directly over the meat.
6. After a further 20 minutes, the lamb will be ready.
7. Peel and wash the potatoes. Cut them into slices of approximately half a cm thick.
8. Sauté the potatoes in a frying pan with plenty of oil. Cook over a low heat. When they are cooked, turn the heat up and finish frying until golden brown.
9. Serve the lamb with the potatoes.

Roast Lamb

Fillet of Pork

with Apple Fritters

Pork fillet for 4

4 Golden Delicious apples

Single cream

Mustard

Salt

Pepper

A little flour

METHOD FOR 4

1. Slice the apples and coat with flour.
2. Heat plenty of olive oil in a pan and fry the apple slices until soft. Remove and set aside.
3. Next, cut the pork fillet, season and fry in the same oil used for frying the apples until golden.
4. When ready, place the fillets on individual plates and serve with the apple fritters.
5. Pour off some of the oil from the pan. Add the cream and mustard according to taste. Return to heat and when the sauce is ready, pour it over the fillets.

Fillet of Pork with Apple Fritters

Sirloin Steak with Smoked Cheese Sauce

4 sirloin steaks

1/2 litre single cream

1/2 litre milk

250 g smoked cheese (Idiazábal)

Salt

Pepper

METHOD FOR 4

1. Melt the cheese in a pan over a low heat. Add the milk and the cream.
2. Cook very slowly for 15 minutes until the sauce is totally blended. Remove from the heat. Strain the sauce to remove any lumps.
3. Season the steaks with salt and pepper. Fry in a pan over a high heat until golden brown on both sides.
4. Heat the oven.
5. Put the steaks in an oven dish. Pour the sauce over and cook for 2 or 3 minutes on low.

1 chicken
Salt
Flour
1 dl of olive oil
3 onions
2 ripe tomatoes
4 dried peppers
1 glass of white wine
Meat stock

Chicken in Tomato Sauce

(Pollo al chilindrón)

METHOD FOR 4

1. Chop the chicken into pieces. Season and coat with flour.
2. Heat the oil in a pan. Stir-fry the chicken pieces over a high heat.
3. Put the oil used for frying the chicken in another pan and fry the chopped onions. When they begin to turn golden, add the peeled and crushed tomatoes and the soaked peppers.
4. When the tomato is ready, add a glass of white wine and leave to cook for a further 10 minutes.
5. Crush the tomato sauce in a blender. Put the chicken pieces in another pan along with the tomato sauce.
6. Leave to cook slowly, adding the stock until the chicken is tender.

Meatballs with Vegetables in Sauce

1 kg mince

250 g peas (frozen or tinned)

2 eggs

2 cloves of garlic

Baby carrots

1 leek

$1/2$ glass of white wine

Breadcrumbs

Flour

$1/2$ litre of water

1 meat stock cube

Olive oil

1 bay leaf

Parsley

Pepper

Salt

METHOD FOR 4

1. In a bowl mix the mince, the chopped cloves of garlic and parsley, the eggs, the breadcrumbs, the salt, the pepper and some of the white wine.
2. Stir all the ingredients until well blended.
3. Make meatballs, coating them with flour. Fry in a pan with oil.
4. Remove the meatballs from the pan and set aside. Use the same oil to sauté the chopped leek, baby carrots and bay leaf.
5. When soft, add the rest of the white wine, the water, the crumbled stock cube, the meatballs and the peas.
6. Season and cook for 20 minutes over a low heat to blend the flavours.

Meatballs with Vegetables in Sauce

Partridge, La Mancha-Style

4 partridges
A little cinnamon
Salt
Piece of cured ham
2 cloves of garlic
3 tablesp. olive oil
20 g lard
1 small glass of white wine
1 bay leaf
Thyme

METHOD FOR 4

1. Clean the partridges carefully and dry well. Season with salt, pepper and a little cinnamon.
2. Chop the ham into tiny pieces.
3. Peel and chop the cloves of garlic.
4. Heat the oil and lard in a large pan. Brown the partridges on both sides.
5. Remove and put them in another pan. Set to one side.
6. In the same fat, sauté the ham, the garlic, the bay leaf and the thyme.
7. Pour this mixture over the partridges and add the glass of white wine.
8. Cover the pan with a plate of water and cook over a very low heat. Stir frequently with a wooden spoon, watching that the food doesn't stick to the bottom of the pan.
9. When the partridge meat is tender, strain the sauce. Pour the sauce over the partridges to serve.

Partridge, La Mancha-Style

Rabbit Stewed in Cider

1 rabbit
3 carrots
3 potatoes
3 parsnips
100 g butter
25 g pine nuts
1 teasp. corn flour
2 onions
150 g fat bacon
4 tablesp. oil
1 bouquet garni
3 cloves of garlic
1 1/2 glasses of cider
Salt
Pepper

METHOD FOR 4

1. Peel and chop the carrots, the potatoes and the parsnips into equal-sized pieces. Heat 50 g of butter in a pan and sauté the vegetables. Set to one side.
2. Take the rabbit's liver and crush it together with the pine nuts. Blend with the corn flour dissolved in a little of the cider.
3. Clean the rabbit well and chop.
4. Cut the onions into quarters.
5. Dice the bacon and sauté in a saucepan with 25 g of butter. Remove from pan and add the rest of the butter and the oil. Brown the rabbit pieces and the onions. Season with salt and pepper.
6. Add the bouquet garni, the cloves of garlic, the cider and the fried bacon. Cover the pan and leave to cook over a low heat.
7. After 1 hour, add the sautéed vegetables, the liver paste and pine nuts.
8. Cook for a further 20 minutes. Serve hot.

4 sirloin steaks weighing 250 g each

150 g mushrooms

1 tablesp. butter

1 dl of meat stock

1/2 dl single cream

1 tablesp. flour

1 tablesp. olive oil

1 small glass of sweet red wine

Salt

Pepper

Braised Sirloin Steak

with Mushroom Sauce

METHOD FOR 4

1. Chop the mushrooms. Melt a little of the butter in a pan and sauté the mushrooms.
2. Add the stock and cream. Cook for about 5 minutes.
3. Remove pan from heat. Blend and season the sauce. Set aside.
4. Season the steaks and coat with flour. Braise in a pan with hot oil and the rest of the butter.
5. Remove the steaks and carefully flame the pan with the wine. Pour in the sauce and bring it to boiling point. Strain.
6. Arrange the steaks on a serving dish and pour the sauce over.

Ham Shank with Turnip Greens

(Lacón con grelos)

4 ham shanks

2 bunches of turnip greens

4 chorizo sausages

Lard

METHOD FOR 4

1. Desalt the shanks by soaking them in water 2 - 3 days before cooking.
2. Cook the shanks in a pan with plenty of water for 3 hours. Once they are cooked, set the water to one side for cooking the other ingredients.
3. Rinse the turnip top leaves well, making sure to get rid of any soil.
4. Cook the turnip top leaves and chorizo sausages in the water used for cooking the ham shanks, adding a little lard.
5. Finally, put the ham shanks on a serving dish. Garnish with the turnip top leaves and chorizo sausages.

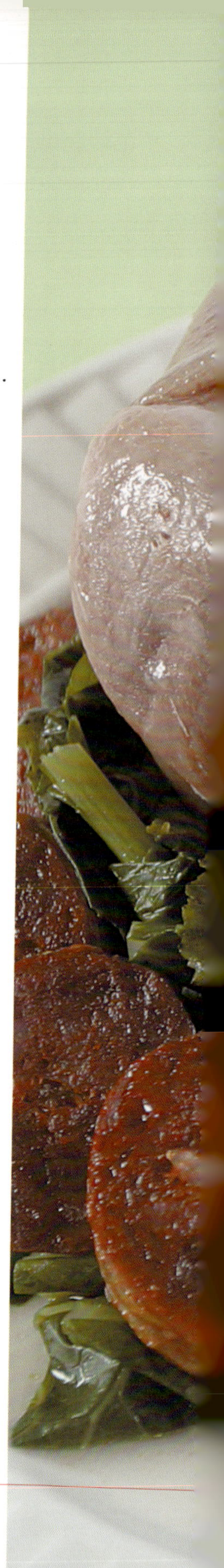

Lacón con grelos

Oxtail Stew with Beans

1 kg ox tail

1/2 kg beans

Unrefined salt

1 or 2 onions

1 tomato

4 bay leaves

1 or 2 cloves of garlic

1 tablesp. sweet paprika

2 dl of red wine

1/2 litre of water

1 tablesp. salt

METHOD FOR 4

1. The previous night, soak the beans in lukewarm water and unrefined salt.
2. Peel and chop the onion.
3. Heat the oil in a frying pan. Sauté the onion carefully, making sure it doesn't burn.
4. Wash, peel and crush the tomato.
5. Chop the ox tail and add it to the pan together with the tomato and 2 of the bay leaves. Braise for 10 minutes.
6. Peel and chop the garlic.
7. Add the garlic, the paprika (making sure it doesn't burn), the glass of red wine and the water to the pan. Simmer for 30 minutes.
8. Add the beans and the 2 bay leaves. Cook for another hour.
9. Season with 1 tablespoonful of salt.
10. Finally, serve hot.

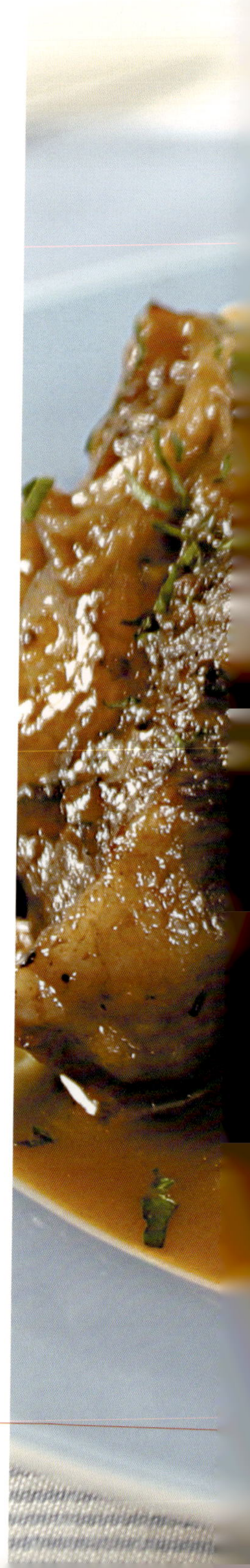

Oxtail Stew with Beans

Fish Dishes

Fried Fillet of Sole in Breadcrumbs

4 soles

Red cabbage leaves

2 eggs

100 g breadcrumbs

1 clove of garlic

Parsley

Lemon

1/2 litre of olive oil

Salt

METHOD FOR 4

1. Fillet the soles. Rinse and dab dry with a napkin.
2. Wash the red cabbage leaves carefully and dab dry with a napkin. Arrange the leaves on a serving dish in the shape of a leaf.
3. Beat the eggs in a bowl with a pinch of salt. Put some breadcrumbs on a plate. Season the sole fillets and coat them first with the beaten egg and then with the breadcrumbs.
4. Heat the oil in a pan. When the oil is very hot, fry the coated fish until golden. Drain well on kitchen paper. Set to one side and keep warm.
5. Slice the clove of garlic. Pour off most of the oil used for frying the fish and fry the garlic until golden.
6. Arrange the fish on the red cabbage leaves. Garnish with the fried garlic, chopped parsley and slices of lemon.

Fried Fillet of Sole in Breadcrumbs

Baked Salmon

4 salmon steaks, weighing
250 g each
Flour
150 g butter
Lard
1 glass of white wine
1 glass of fish stock
Salt
Potatoes
4 tomatoes

METHOD FOR 4

1. Salt the salmon steaks and coat lightly with flour.
2. Melt the butter and lard in a pan. Fry the salmon steaks a little on both sides. Remove from pan and set the fat to one side.
3. Pour the sauce into an oven dish. Add the salmon, the wine and the fish stock. Place in a preheated oven at 200°C for approximately 4 or 5 minutes.
4. Take out the salmon steaks. Remove skin and bones and put them into the dish in which the salmon was baked. Arrange the steaks on a serving dish and set to one side.
5. Mix the skin and bones with the sauce. Strain and pour it over the salmon steaks.
6. Serve accompanied with fried tomatoes and boiled potatoes.

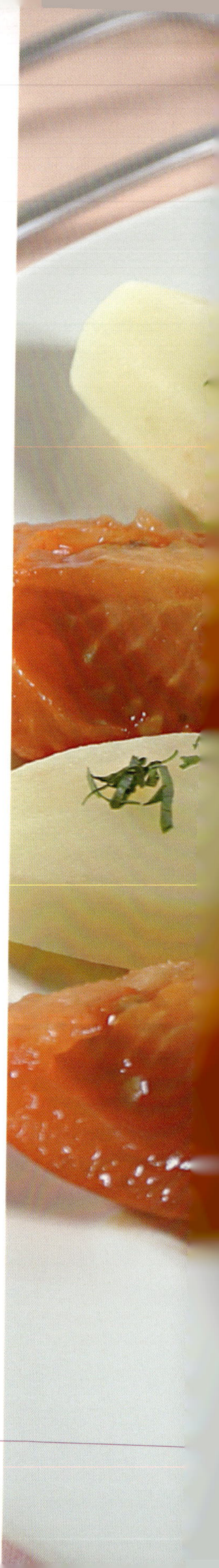

Baked Salmon

Baked Cod, Cantabrian-Style

500 g cured cod
2 onions
2 cloves of garlic
1 lemon
Parsley
200 g flour
1 dl of white wine
2 dl of water
3 dl of olive oil
Salt

METHOD FOR 4

1. The day before, soak the cod, changing the water several times.
2. Cut the cod into squares and coat with flour. Set to one side.
3. Chop the onions finely.
4. Heat the oil in a pan. Sauté the onion, making sure it doesn't burn. Add a tablespoonful of flour and stir well.
5. Pour in the wine and cook for 5 minutes.
6. Crush the garlic and a sprig of parsley with a pestle and mortar. Mix with a little lemon juice and add to the pan.
7. Mix all the ingredients well and pour over the fish.

- 1 $1/2$ kg squid
- $1/2$ kg onions
- $1/2$ kg tomatoes
- 7 tablesp. olive oil
- Bread
- 1 tablesp. flour
- 2 cloves of garlic
- Parsley
- Salt

Baby Squid Stewed in Its Own Ink

(Chipirones en su tinta)

METHOD FOR 4

1. Clean the squid well, carefully removing the ink sacs. Remove the fins and tentacles.
2. Chop 1 onion finely. Heat the oil in a frying pan and sauté the onion until golden, together with the chopped garlic and parsley. Cook over a low heat and add the tomatoes (peeled).
3. Stuff the squid with their fins and tentacles and secure with a cocktail stick. Sauté them, then cover and cook for 1 hour.
4. After half an hour, add the ink (strained) and the tablespoonful of flour (toasted). Simmer for another 30 minutes.
5. Take the squid out of the pan. Remove the cocktail sticks. Put the squid in a dish. Strain the sauce and pour it over the squid.
6. Fry a few pieces of bread and use to garnish the dish.

Hake with Prawns & Cream

1 kg hake

Flour

1/2 head of garlic

1/2 litre of cream

1/2 litre of concentrated fish stock (fumet)

400 g prawns

2 dl of olive oil

Salt

METHOD FOR 4

1. Clean the hake, removing the head and bones. Cut into fillets. Coat the fillets with flour.
2. Slice the garlic. Heat oil in a pan and fry the garlic, taking care that it doesn't burn.
3. When it starts to turn golden, add the hake, skin-side up.
4. When the fish is golden, turn it over and add the cream and the concentrated fish stock.
5. Cook for a few minutes, stirring continuously. Remove from heat.
6. Put the hake in an oven dish. Add some stock from the pan and the shrimps. Place in a pre-heated medium oven for approximately 5 minutes to brown.

Hake with Prawns & Cream

Monkfish Stew with Clams

800 g monkfish
3 cloves of garlic
Parsley
Flour
3 eggs
1 can of asparagus
250 g clams
3 dl of olive oil
Pepper
Salt

METHOD FOR 4

1. Clean the monkfish, cut into slices and season.
2. Crush the cloves of garlic and the parsley with a pestle and mortar and spread them over the fish. Leave to macerate for approximately 30 minutes.
3. Next, coat the fish with flour and beaten egg.
4. Heat the oil in a pan. Fry the fish, drain and set to one side.
5. Open the can of asparagus. Drain, keeping the brine.
6. Pour a little of the oil used for frying the monkfish into a heatproof earthenware dish. Add a tablespoonful of flour. Stir well to prevent any lumps from forming and add the brine from the asparagus.
7. Clean the clams well, getting rid of any sand. Discard any whose shells are broken or which don't close when handling.
8. Add the monkfish and clams to the pan. Stir until the sauce thickens and the clams have opened up. Leave to cook for a further 10 minutes.
9. When the sauce is ready, cut the asparagus and add to the pan.

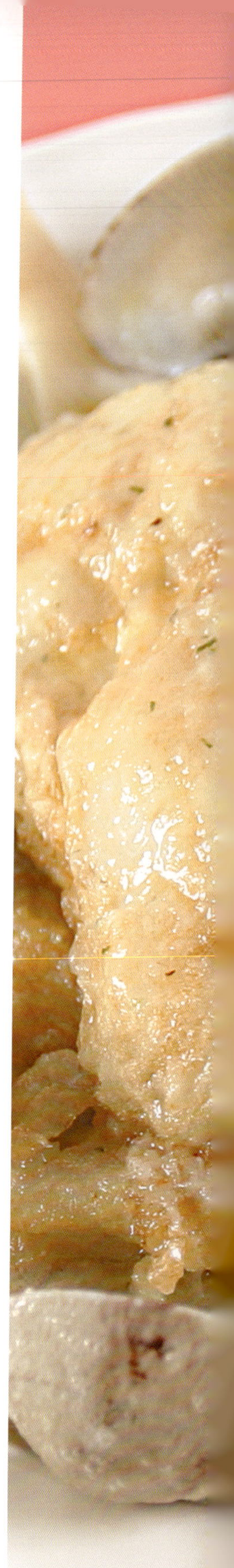

Monkfish Stew with Clams

Sea Bass in a Salt Crust

1 sea bass weighing 1 kg

1 kg of unrefined salt

METHOD FOR 4

1. Wash the fish, but do not remove either scales or guts so that the salt will not penetrate inside the fish.
2. Arrange a layer of salt the size of the fish on an oven tray. Place the fish on top of the salt. Put another layer of salt over the fish until it is completely covered.
3. Dampen the salt to make it compact.
4. Heat the oven to approximately 190°C and put the fish in.
5. Wait 20 minutes until the salt forms a hard crust. Remove from the oven.
6. With the help of a serrated knife, cut the salt crust. Cut the fish into fillets, taking care that they don't come apart. Discard the head and bones.
7. Arrange the fillets on individual plates. Serve with olive oil, mayonnaise, vinaigrette or Tartar sauce.

500 g cured cod
400 g onions
600 g ripe tomatoes
2 red peppers
3 cloves of garlic
3 dried sweet red peppers
1 bay leaf
60 g flour
Breadcrumbs
3 dl of oil
Parsley

Cod, Basque-Style

(Bacalao a la vizcaína)

METHOD FOR 4

1. 24 hours before, soak the cod to desalt it, changing the water up to 4 times.
2. Roast the peppers and remove skin when cool.
3. Soak the dried peppers in lukewarm water for about 30 minutes.
4. Put the drained cod into a pan with a little water, the bay leaf and the parsley. Bring to the boil.
5. Remove the cod from the pan. Take out the bones. Coat with flour and fry lightly in plenty of hot oil. Set to one side.
6. Slice the onions. Sauté in a pan with a little oil. Before the onion starts turning brown, add the chopped parsley and garlic. Add the tomatoes (peeled and deseeded), the dried pepper pulp and cook until the tomato juice has been absorbed.
7. Once the sauce is ready, pour a little into an oven dish. Place the fried cod pieces on top and cover with the rest of the sauce.
8. Slice the peppers into strips. Use them to garnish the fish. Sprinkle with breadcrumbs mixed with chopped parsley. Place under the grill for 10 minutes.

Baked Sea Bream

4 sea bream

Fish stock

1 onion

2 ripe tomatoes

4 dried peppers

Paprika

4 leaves of Swiss chard leaves

3 cloves of garlic

Pine nuts

Parsley

Pepper

4 medium-sized potatoes

Olive oil

Salt

METHOD FOR 4

1. Clean the fish well, removing the head and bones. Cut in half lengthwise.
2. To make stock, put some water in a pan together with the head and the bones and cook. Drain and set to one side.
3. Chop the onion and garlic finely.
4. Wash and chop the tomatoes.
5. Soak the dried peppers in water.
6. Heat the oil in a pan. Sauté the onion, the garlic, the tomato, the paprika, the pulp from the soaked dried peppers and a little fish stock.
7. Peel and wash the potatoes.
8. Chop the Swiss chard. Cook in a pan with water. Add the pine nuts and season according to taste.
9. Place the fish in an oven dish. Add the potatoes and season.
10. Place in a preheated oven at 170°C and bake for 15 minutes.
11. Place the fish on a serving dish. Pour the tomato sauce over. Sprinkle with chopped parsley. Garnish with little balls made with the Swiss chard and pine nuts (after draining well).

Baked Sea Bream

Marinated Fried Fish

1 kg fish
1 clove of garlic
Paprika
Oregano
Ground pepper
Flour
Olive oil
Salt

METHOD FOR 4

1. Clean the fish well, removing the skin and bones.
2. Cut into medium-sized pieces and place in a dish.
3. Peel the clove of garlic and crush with a pestle and mortar.
4. Season the fish with salt and pepper, paprika, the crushed garlic and a little oregano. Drizzle with oil.
5. Stir well so that the marinade will coat all the fish well. Leave to marinate a few hours to allow the flavour to develop.
6. Finally, take out the fish pieces, drain and coat with flour.
7. Heat plenty of oil in a frying pan. Deep-fry the fish until golden. Serve garnished with lemon wedges.

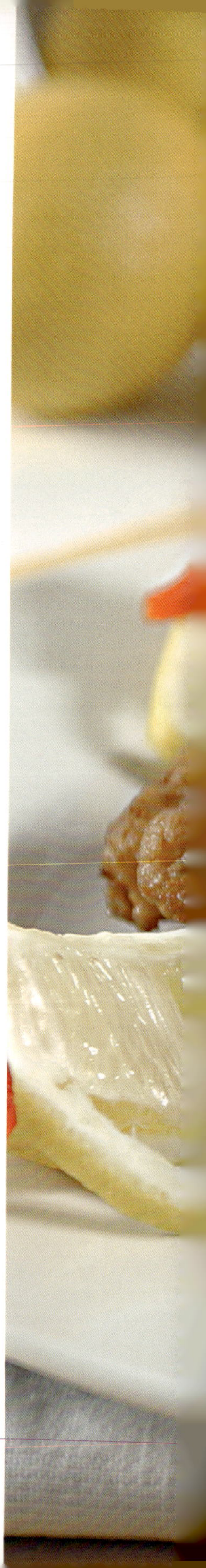

Marinated Fried Fish

Desserts

Custard & Cream Crêpes

(Filloas)

For the crêpes:

6 eggs

75 g flour

1/2 litre of milk

Icing sugar

Butter

For the custard filling:

1/2 litre of milk

100 g sugar

6 egg yolks

50 g flour

Cinnamon stick

1 lemon

Whipped cream

METHOD FOR 4

1. In a bowl, make the crêpe batter by beating the milk, flour and eggs. Melt the butter. Add it together with the salt and beat again. Strain the mixture.

2. Heat a non-stick frying pan. Pour in just enough mixture to coat the bottom of the pan. When the crêpe has set on one side, turn carefully, making sure that it doesn't break. When set on the other side, remove from pan and reserve. Repeat the same procedure until all the crêpes are made.

3. For making the custard filling, put the milk and cinnamon stick in another pan and bring to the boil over a low heat. Set aside to cool.

4. In a bowl, beat the yolks and sugar. When well blended, add the flour dissolved in a little cold milk. Mix with the boiled milk and add the lemon rind. Bring to the boil over a low heat until the custard thickens, taking care that it doesn't boil. Set aside to cool.

5. Fill the crêpes with the custard, rolling each one up. May be garnished with a little whipped cream on each side. Dust with sugar.

Filloas

Apple Pie

3 cooking apples

400 g short crust pastry

10 g butter

1 lemon

Apricot jam

1 kiwi

1 large strawberry

Blackcurrants

Raspberries

Whipped cream

300 g **custard base:**

1/2 litre of milk

100 g sugar

6 egg yolks

50 g flour

Stick of cinnamon

1 lemon

METHOD FOR 4

1. Make the custard by boiling the milk with the cinnamon stick. When the milk starts to boil, remove pan from heat.
2. In a bowl, beat the yolks and sugar. When well blended, add the flour dissolved in a little cold milk. Mix with the boiled milk and add the lemon rind. Bring to the boil over a low heat until the custard thickens, taking care that it doesn't boil. Set aside to cool.
3. Grease a round pie dish with butter and line it with the pastry.
4. Pour in the custard filling.
5. Peel the apples, remove cores and cut into slices of approximately half a centimetre.
6. Drizzle the apple slices with the juice of 1 lemon so that they will not turn brown. Arrange them over the custard filling, making sure that they overlap slightly.
7. Bake for 20 minutes in a preheated oven at 150°C until the apple is golden brown.
8. Remove the pie from the oven. Glaze with the jam.
9. Decorate the pie with the rest of the fruit. Serve with whipped cream.

Apple Pie

Cantabrian Cheesecake

(Quesada pasiega)

250 g flour

50 g sugar

1 egg

1/2 litre milk

15 g butter

2 tablesp. curd/cottage cheese

Grated rind of 1 lemon

1/2 teasp. baking powder

Salt

METHOD FOR 4

1. Beat the egg and sugar in a bowl. Continue beating whilst adding the other ingredients, making sure that there are no lumps.
2. Grease a cake tin with the butter and pour in the previous mixture.
3. Preheat the oven a few minutes at 250°C. Before putting the cheesecake in, turn the temperature down to 225°C. Bake for 30 minutes until golden.
4. Prick with a needle to check if it's ready and when it comes out clean, remove the cheesecake from the oven. Set aside to cool.
5. When cold, remove from tin and garnish with lemon slices (optional).

Quesada pasiega

Torrijas

1 litre of milk

1 stick of cinnamon

Rind of 1 lemon

6 tablesp. sugar

1 stick of French bread (from the previous day)

2 eggs

Olive oil

Ground cinnamon

Sugar

METHOD FOR 4

1. Put the milk, cinnamon stick and lemon rind in a pan. Cook over a low heat for about 5 minutes. Add the sugar and stir until it has dissolved. Set to one side.
2. Cut the bread into slices and place them in a deep dish.
3. Pour the hot milk over the slices, making sure they absorb the milk well.
4. Beat the eggs and coat each slice of bread well.
5. Next, heat the oil and deep fry on both sides, taking care the slices don't break when turning.
6. When they are golden, remove from pan and arrange on a large serving dish.
7. May be served sprinkled with sugar and ground cinnamon or drizzled with syrup or honey.

Torrijas

Baked Custard with Caramelised Topping

(Crema Catalana)

$1/2$ litre of milk

Rind of 1 lemon

1 stick of cinnamon

300 g corn flour

6 egg yolks

9 tablesp. sugar

100 g sugar for making caramel sauce

METHOD FOR 4

1. Set aside a little of the milk in a bowl for dissolving the corn flour. Pour the rest preferably into an earthenware dish.
2. Wash and peel a lemon. Add the rind to the milk along with the stick of cinnamon. Bring to the boil and remove from heat.
3. Make a paste by dissolving the corn flour in the milk.
4. Next, with a mixer beat the egg yolks and sugar until creamy.
5. Strain the milk. Add the corn flour and yolks, beating well.
6. Put the pan over a low heat, stirring continuously. Do not boil, since the mixture would curdle.
7. When it thickens a little, remove from the heat.
8. Continue stirring whilst pouring the custard into individual bowls. Leave to cool.
9. Before serving, sprinkle the custard with sugar. Caramelise the sugar by burning it with a special hot rod.

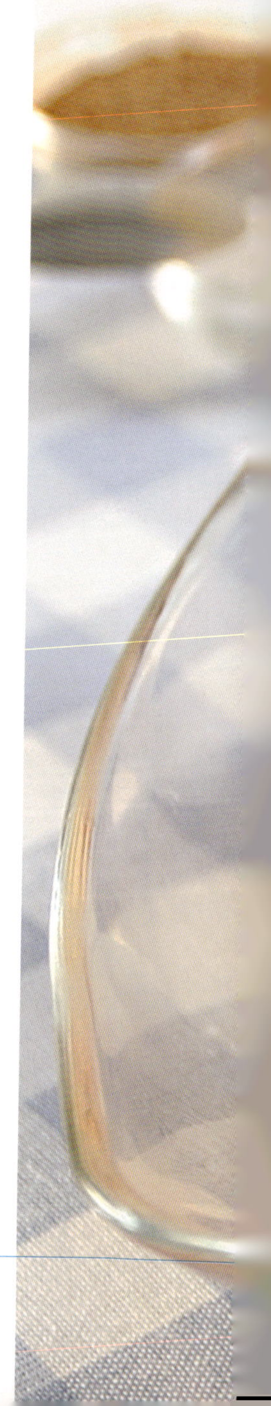

Crema catalana

Chocolate Millefeuille

400 g chocolate

400 g flaky pastry

1 dl of Gran Marnier

200 g butter

75 g sugar

Blackcurrants

Blackberries

METHOD FOR 4

1. Preheat the oven to 150°C and bake 4 sheets of flaky pastry for 15 minutes.
2. Remove the pastry from the oven and drizzle with Gran Marnier.
3. Melt the chocolate in a pan.
4. Mix the butter with 75 g of sugar and beat into a creamy consistency. Spread this mixture over each sheet of pastry and wait until it hardens.
5. Pour a thin layer of melted chocolate over the first sheet. Place another one on top of the chocolate and repeat with the other 3 layers.
6. Coat with the rest of the chocolate.
7. Leave to cool until the chocolate hardens.
8. Decorate with the blackcurrants and blackberries.